William Milford Giffin

Suggestive Opening Exercises for Schools

William Milford Giffin

Suggestive Opening Exercises for Schools

ISBN/EAN: 9783743417212

Manufactured in Europe, USA, Canada, Australia, Japa

Cover: Foto ©Paul-Georg Meister /pixelio.de

Manufactured and distributed by brebook publishing software
(www.brebook.com)

William Milford Giffin

Suggestive Opening Exercises for Schools

SUGGESTIVE

OPENING EXERCISES

FOR SCHOOLS.

—BY—

WILLIAM M. GIFFIN, A. M.

NEW YORK:
TEACHERS' PUBLISHING CO.
18 ASTOR PLACE, N. Y.
1889.

INTRODUCTION.

During a long experience in the school-room, the author has had an opportunity to test the desirability of making the school attractive. The more cheerful the school and its surroundings the happier are the children. Happy children are seldom, if ever, malicious or unmanageable. When the malicious and unmanageable element is removed, more than one half of the teachers's work has been done.

We often see in school journals the questions (1) "How shall I prevent tardiness?" (2) "Will you please tell me how to increase my attendance?" (3) "Can you give a teacher of a country school any hints for conducting general exercises?" (4) "Do you know of any good biblical selections for school exercises?" Who has not seen just such questions time and again? It is a great satisfaction to know that they are asked. Such questions simply prove that our young teachers are interested in their work and are desirous of obtaining the experience of others who have had longer and perhaps better opportunities than they.

The purpose of this little book is to answer just such questions in as practical a way as possible. The author has given many exercises that he has seen used in the class room and hence he knows what their true value is. Nothing theoretical is given. They are simple little exercises in which the children delight, and which take no great time or talent to teach.

The author by using them for his opening exercises, has made that period of the day so entertaining and instructive to the children, that none of the pupils desire to be absent from it, and hence he has but very few cases of absence or tardiness to record.

If devotional exercises are arranged with skill and therefore, are apropos, they must win and hold the attention of the children and of necessity, teach their lesson. But few are given here, as it was not thought advisable to make too large or costly a book ; so that all might feel able to procure one. A sufficient number, it is thought are given, to suggest to the young teachers the fact that this portion of their programme, by a little study on their part, can have an aim and influence for good. No doubt, many who read the devotional exercises given here, will be made to realize for the first time, that there is a fit time and place for particular biblical selections, just as there is a fit time and place for every other exercise found on their programme.

A lady who once witnessed the " Eastern Wind Storm" and "Western Cyclone," wrote of them as follows : "One of our eastern wind-storms was called for, and as the teacher increased or diminished the distance between his extended hands, the storm raged and lulled. It was made by the production of various hissing and rustling sounds which, blended, made a very good imitation of the wind. Then a western cyclone was invited, and it came like—like a cyclone. Its force was regulated by the hands of the teacher as easily as he had controlled the lesser tempest. I mentally summed up the benefits of the exercise as follows : Habits cultivated ; attention and responsiveness ; idea of modulation developed, and a point in climate taught ; economy of pedagogical effort by the utilization of recreation and physical exercise in adding thus to mental growth ; principle of indirect teaching illustrated, while the mind is pleasurably intent upon one idea, others are slipping in unawares."

Hence, to say one has not time for such exercise, is simply to say he has not time to teach. These exercises may be made just as educative as the conning of definitions from a text book. We have sometimes thought they were more valuable.

Trusting that my readers may find much profit and pleasure in them, I leave the little book in the hands of my *professional* friends throughout the union.   WM. M. G.

Newark, N. J.

DEVOTIONAL EXERCISES.

I.

The XXIV Psalm when rendered as here given is very impressive. The italicised words are for emphasis. One of the older pupils, if a good reader, may take the part assigned to the teacher.

TEACHER.

The earth is the Lord's, and the fullness thereof; the world, and they that dwell therein.

For He hath founded it upon the seas, and established it upon the floods.

Who shall ascend into the hill of the Lord? or who shall stand in his *holy* place?

PUPILS.

He that hath *clean hands*, and a *pure heart;* who hath not lifted up his soul unto vanity nor sworn deceitfully.

He shall receive the blessing from the Lord, and righteousness from the God of his salvation.

This is the generation of them that seek him, that seek *thy* face, O Jacob.

TEACHER.

Lift up your heads, *O ye gates;* and be ye lifted up,

ye *everlasting doors*; and the King of *glory* shall come in.

PUPILS.

Who *is* this King of glory?

TEACHER.

The Lord *strong and mighty*, the Lord mighty in battle. Lift up your heads, O ye gates; even lift them up, ye everlasting doors *and the King of glory shall come in.*

PUPILS.

Who is this King of glory?

TEACHER.

The Lord of hosts, *he* is the King of glory. Selah.

LORD'S PRAYER.

HYMN. *(Dennis.)*

Father, who art in heaven,
  O, hallowed be Thy name:
Thy kingdom come: Thy will be done
  On earth in Heaven the same.

Give us this day our bread,
  Forgive us each his debt;
As we forgive our debtors, Lord,
  Let us thy judgment get.

O, tempt us not to-day,
  But keep our thoughts from sin;
For Thine's the kingdom and the power,
  The glory forever, Amen.

The words in the last verse, last line, should not be slurred.

II.

The same Psalm, with the XXIII, may also be given as below. If there is but one room, the parts assigned to the different classes may be given to the different rows of pupils. The author has six classes on one floor, and hence, has it rendered as here printed. The hymn which follows the Psalm was taken from the "American Teacher."

FIRST CLASS.

The Lord is *my* shepherd, *I* shall not want;
He maketh me to lie down in green pastures : he leadeth me beside the still waters.

SECOND CLASS.

He restoreth my soul : he leadeth me in the paths of righteousness for his name's sake.

THIRD CLASS.

Yea, though I walk through the valley of the shadow of *death*, I will fear no evil: for Thou art with me, Thy rod and Thy staff, they comfort me.

FOURTH CLASS.

Thou preparest a table before me in the presence of mine enemies, Thou anointest my head with oil; my cup runneth over.

FIFTH CLASS.

Surely, goodness and mercy shall follow me all the days of my life, and I shall dwell in the house of the Lord forever.

SIXTH CLASS.

The earth is the Lord's, and the fullness thereof; the world, and they that dwell therein. For he hath founded it upon the seas, and established it upon the floods.

TEACHER.

Who shall ascend into the hill of the Lord ? or who shall stand in his holy place ?

ALL THE PUPILS.

He that hath *clean hands* and a *pure heart* ; who hath not lifted up his soul unto vanity, nor sworn deceitfully.

He shall receive the blessing from the Lord, and righteousness from the God of his salvation.

This is is the generation of them that seek him, that seek *thy* face, O, Jacob.

TEACHER.

Lift up your heads, *O ye gates* ; and be ye lifted up, ye *everlasting doors* ; and the King of *glory* shall come in.

PUPILS.

Who *is* this King of glory ?

TEACHER.

The Lord *strong and mighty*, the Lord mighty in battle.

Lift up your heads, O ye gates ; even lift them up, ye everlasting doors *and the King of glory shall come in.*

PUPILS.

Who is this King of glory ?

TEACHER.

The Lord of hosts *he* is the King of glory. Selah.

LORD'S PRAYER.

HYMN. *(Manoah.)*

I thank thee Lord, for quiet rest,
   And for Thy care of me :
Oh let me thro' this day be blest,
   And kept from harm by Thee.

Oh let me thank Thee, kind Thou art,
   To children such as I :
Give me a gentle loving heart,
   Be Thou my friend on high.

Help me to please my teachers dear,
   And do whate'er they tell :
Bless all my friends both far and near,
   And keep them safe and well.

III.

After announcing the death of a pupil to the school the following opening exercises will be found very impressive. If one of the teachers or older girls sings the little hymn it will add to the effect.

The brevity of the exercises is to be commended. The hymn is taken from, " Bright Jewels," p. 131.

TEACHER.

In a calm deliberate tone.

Suffer little children to come unto me and forbid them *not*, for of such is the kingdom of heaven.

LORD'S PRAYER.

HYMN.

Gone to the grave is our loved one,
  Gone with a youthful bloom ;
Lowly we bend, schoolmate and friend
  Passing away to the tomb.

Chorus. They are going down the valley,
  The deep, dark valley ;
We'll see their faces never more,
  Till we pass down the valley,
The dark, death valley,
  And meet them on the other shore.

O'ft we have mingled together,
  Sometimes in prayer and song ;
Now when we meet, this one we greet
  Never again in our throng.   Cho.

Or if preferred the school may sing the following hymn.

Shall we gather at the river
  Where bright angel feet have trod ;
With its crystal tide forever
  Flowing by the throne of God ?

Chorus. Yes, we'll gather at the river,
  The beautiful, the beautiful river
Gather with the saints at the river
  That flows by the throne of God.

Soon we'll reach the shining river,
  Soon our pilgrimage will cease ;
Soon our happy hearts will quiver
  With the melody of peace.   *Cho.*

IV.

Oftentimes teachers are called upon to solicit alms from the school; as, at the time of the Chicage fire, the Southern floods etc. If, after such solicitations the following verses bearing on the subject are read, it will be the right selection in the right place.

TEACHER.

Blessed is he that considereth the poor : the Lord will deliver him in time of trouble.

The Lord will preserve him, and keep him alive ; and he shall be blessed upon the earth : and thou wilt not deliver him unto the will of his enemies.

The Lord will strengthen him upon the bed of languishing : thou wilt make all his bed in his sickness.

Blessed be the Lord God of Israel from everlasting and to everlasting. Amen and Amen. XLI Psalm.

LORD'S PRAYER.

HYMN. *(Stephens.)*

Let children hear the mighty deeds,
Which God performed of old,
Which in our younger years we saw,
And which our fathers told.

Thus they shall learn, in God alone,
Their hope securely stands,
That they may ne'er forget his works
But practice his commands.

(Song Garden.)

This may be sung by the school or recited by a little girl.

Or the following selection from James I : 22 to 27 inclusive is very apropos to such occasions.

TEACHER.

But be ye *doers* of the word, and not *hearers* only, deceiving your own selves. For if any be a *hearer* of the word, and *not* a *doer*, he is like unto a man beholding his natural face in a glass! For he beholdeth himself, and goeth his way, and straightway forgetteth what manner of man he was.

But whoso *looketh* into the perfect law of liberty, and *continueth therein, he* being *not* a *forgetful hearer but* a *doer* of the *work*, this man shall be blessed in his deed.

If any man among you seem to be religious, and bridleth not his tongue, but deceiveth his own heart, this man's religion is vain.

Pure religion and undefiled, before God and the Father is *this*, To *visit* the *fatherless* and *widows* in their *affliction*, and to keep himself *unspotted* from the world.

LORD'S PRAYER.

HYMN.

(*Here's to Good Old Yale.*)

When you find a noble cause,
Help it on!
When you find a noble cause,
Help it on!
Never wait for man's applause,
Never count the cost, nor pause,
Help it on, help it on,
Help it on, on, on!

(*Happy Voices.*)

The following verses from St. Matthew would also be appropriate.

Not every one that saith unto me, LORD, LORD, shall enter into the kingdom of heaven ; but he that *doeth* the *will* of my Father which is in heaven.

Many will say to me in that day, LORD, LORD, have we not *prophesied* in thy name? and in thy name have *cast out devils?* and in thy name done *many wonderful works?*

And then will I profess unto them, *I never knew you; depart* from me, ye that work iniquity. Therefore, whosoever *heareth* these sayings of mine, and *doeth* them, I will liken him unto a *wise* man, which built his house upon a rock. And the rain descended, and the floods came, and the winds blew, and beat upon that house ; and it *fell not*; for it was founded upon a rock.

And every one that *heareth* these sayings of mine, and doeth them *not*, shall be likened unto a *foolish* man, which built his house upon the sand.

And the rain descended, and the floods came, and the winds blew, and beat upon that house ; and it *fell*; and *great* was the *fall* of *it*.

V.

For many years the author has made it a practice to ask his pupils each to bring one potato at least to school on the day before Thanksgiving.

From a school of between six and seven hundred pupils, he has received as many as ten barrels which were distributed among the poor families of the district or ward.

After such a donation a few verses from the CIII Psalm will be appropriate. (See page 14.)

TEACHER.

Bless the Lord, O my soul ; and all that is within me, bless his holy name.

Bless the Lord, O my soul, and forget not all his benefits.

Who forgiveth all thine iniquities ; who healeth all thy diseases ; who redeemeth thy life from destruction ; who crowneth thee with loving-kindness and tender mercies ; who satisfieth thy mouth with good things ; so that thy youth is renewed like the eagle's.

PUPILS.

The Lord executed righteousness and judgment for all that are oppressed.

He made known his ways unto Moses, his acts unto the children of Israel.

The Lord is merciful and gracious, slow to anger, and plenteous in mercy.

TEACHER.

To such as keep his covenant, and to those that remember his commandments to do them.

The Lord hath prepared his throne in the heavens; and his kingdom ruleth over all.

Bless the Lord, ye his angels that excel in strength, that do his commandments, harkening unto the voice of his word.

Bless ye the Lord, all ye his hosts ; ye ministers of his that do his pleasure.

Bless the Lord, all his works in all places of his dominion : bless the Lord, O my soul.

LORD'S PRAYER.

HYMN.   *(Allegretto.)*

Oh, bless the Lord, my soul !
  Let all within me join,
And aid my tongue to bless his name,
  Whose favors are divine.

He crowns my life with love,
  When ransomed from the grave ;
He, who redeemed my soul from hell,
  Hath sovereign power to save.

(The Triumph.)

VI.

Children very much dislike long sermons from either parents or teachers. Our recollection of such sermons is that they did but little, if any, good. We also question the propriety of inflicting corporal punishment for swearing. If a teacher by chance, hear a boy swear in the school yard, it is, in our judgment, better to say nothing more than to express surprise and pain, and, at the opening exercises, read from Sts. Matthew and Mark the selections here given, and after school talk to the boy, *from the heart*, impressing upon his mind not only the sinfulness of his own act, but the influence it may have upon others. Never despair if you do not see immediate results. You may never know the influence you have exerted for good.

TEACHER.

Again, ye have heard that it hath been said by them of old time. Thou shalt not forswear thyself, but shalt perform unto the Lord thine oaths.

But I say unto you, Swear not at all ; neither by heaven ; for it is God's throne.

Nor by the earth ; for it is his foot-stool ; neither by Jerusalem ; for it is the city of the great King.

Neither shalt thou swear by thy head, because thou canst not make one hair white or black.

Verily, I say unto you, all sin shall be forgiven unto the sons of men, and blasphemies wherewith soever they shall blaspheme ; but he that shall blaspheme against the Holy Ghost, hath never forgiveness, but is in danger of eternal damnation.

LORD'S PRAYER.

HYMN.

VII.

Let the children commit the parts assigned to them and recite them in the order indicated.

TEACHER.

And seeing the multitudes, he went up into a mountain : and when he was set, his disciples came unto him.

And he opened his mouth ; and taught them, saying. Blessed are the poor in spirit :

PUPILS.

For theirs is the kingdom of heaven.

TEACHER.

Blessed are they that mourn.

PUPILS.

For they shall be comforted.

TEACHER.

Blessed are the meek.

PUPILS.

For they shall inherit the earth.

TEACHER.

Blessed are they which do hunger and thirst after righteousness.

PUPILS.

For they shall be filled.

TEACHER.

Blessed are the merciful.

PUPILS.

For they shall obtain mercy.

TEACHER.

Blessed are the pure in heart:

PUPILS.

For they shall see God.

TEACHER.

Blessed are the peace-makers :

PUPILS.

For they shall be called the children of God.

TEACHER.

Blessed are they which are persecuted for righteousness' sake : for theirs is the kingdom of heaven.

Blessed are ye when men shall revile you, and persecute you, and shall say all manner of evil against you falsely, for my sake.

Rejoice, and be exceeding glad : for great is your reward in heaven : for so persecuted they the prophets which were before you.

LORD'S PRAYER.

HYMN.

Blest are the pure in heart,
　For they shall see their God ;
The secret of the Lord is theirs,
　Their soul is his abode.

Still to the lowly soul,
　He doth himself impart ;
And for his temple and his throne
　Selects the pure in heart.

VIII.

If at any time the teacher knows of any little misunderstandings existing between two (or more) pupils she may, without seeming to do so, exert a good influence by a judicious selection for the opening exercises, as for example, the following from Luke VI : 31 and John XII : 134.

TEACHER.

And as *ye* would that men should do to *you*, do *ye* also to them likewise.

For if *ye* love them which love *you, what thank have ye?* for *sinners also love those that love them.*

And if *ye* do good to them *which do good to you,* what *thank* have ye? for *sinners also* do *even* the same.

A *new commandment I* give *unto you,* That ye *love* one another ; *as I* have *loved you,* that *ye also* love one another.

By *this* shall all men *know* that ye *are my disciples,* if ye have *love* one to another.

LORD'S PRAYER.

HYMN.

This is my commandment,
That ye love one another,
That ye love one another,
As I have loved you.
Blessed words of Jesus
We have heard to-day ;
Savior, by thy spirit,
Help us to obey.
May thy love unite us
To the living Vine.
May our hearts enlighten'd
Glow with love divine.
This is my commandment etc.

P. P. Bliss in the Triumph

IX.

The Sunday question is becoming an all important one in this country. Teachers of public schools, however, we think, should

not deliver long sermons or lectures before the school on subjects
of this kind. The following verses if read in a calm even tone,
without note or comment, must leave an impression. If after
the words, "And the evening and the morning were the *sixth*
day," the reader make a short pause the contrast will be more
marked.

TEACHER.

And God said, let there be *light*; and there *was*
light. And God saw the light, that it was good ; and
God divided the light from the darkness. And God
called the light Day, and the darkness he called
Night.

And the *evening* and the *morning* were the *first* day.

And God made the firmament, and divided the
waters which were under the firmament from the
waters which were above the firmament : and it was
so. And God called the firmament Heaven.

And the *evening* and the *morning* were the *second*
day.

And God said, Let the waters under the heaven be
gathered together unto one place, and let the dry land
appear : and it was so. And the earth brought forth
grass and herb yielding seed after his kind, and the
tree yielding fruit whose seed was in itself, after his
kind : and God saw that it was good.

And the *evening* and the *morning* were the *third*
day.

And God made two great lights ; the greater light
to rule the day, and the lesser light to rule the night :
he made the stars also. And God set them in the
firmament of the heaven to give the light upon the
earth. And to rule over the day and over the night,
and to divide the light from the darkness ; and God
saw that it was good.

And the *evening* and the *morning* were the *fourth* day.

And God said, Let the waters bring forth abundantly the moving creature that hath life, and fowl that may fly above the earth in the open firmament o heaven. And God blessed them, saying, Be fruitful, and multiply, and fill the waters in the seas, and let fowl multiply in the earth.

And the *evening* and the *morning* were the *fifth* day.

And God made the beast of the earth after his kind, and cattle after their kind, and everything that creepeth upon the earth after his kind : and God saw that it was good. So God created man in his own image, in the image of God created he him : male and female created he them. And God blessed them and God said unto them, Be fruitful, and multiply, and replenish the earth and subdue it : and have dominion over the fish of the sea and over the fowl of the air, and over every living thing that moveth upon the earth. And God saw everything he had made : and behold, it was *very good.* And the *evening* and the *morning* were the *sixth* day.

*   *   *   *   *   *

Thus—the *heavens* and the *earth* were *finished,* and all the host of them.

And—on the SEVENTH day God *ended* his work which he had made ; and he *rested* on the *seventh* day from *all* his work which he had made.

And God *blessed* the SEVENTH day and sanctified it : *because that in it he had rested from all his work which God created and made.*

LORD'S PRAYER.

HYMN.

MY COUNTRY, 'TIS OF THEE.

1. My country, 'tis of thee,
   Sweet land of liberty,
       Of thee I sing :
   Land where my fathers died,
   Land of the pilgrims' pride,
   From every mountain side
       Let freedom ring !

2. My native country, thee—
   Land of the noble free—
       Thy name I love :
   I love thy rocks and rills,
   Thy woods and templed hills ;
   My heart with rapture thrills
       Like that above.

3. Let music swell the breeze,
   And ring from all the trees
       Sweet freedom's song !
   Let mortal tongues awake
   Let all that breathe partake ;
   Let rocks their silence break,—
       The sound prolong !

4. Our fathers' God to thee.
   Author of liberty,
       To thee we sing :
   Long may our land be bright
   With freedom's holy light ;
   Protect us by thy might,
   Great God our King !

S. F. Smith.

X.

Selections from the Sermon on the Mount are suitable to all occasions. Matthew vi : 5 to 16 is particularly good. Verses 14 and 15 should be read in such a way as to bring out their full meaning.

And *when thou prayest*, thou shalt *not* be as the *hypocrites are* : for *they* love to pray standing in the *synagogues* and in the *corners* of the *streets*, that they may be seen of *men*. Verily I say unto you, *They have their reward*.

But *thou*, when *thou* prayest, enter into thy closet, and when thou hast shut thy door, pray to thy Father which is in secret ; and thy Father which seeth in secret shall reward thee openly.

But when ye pray, use not *vain repetitions*, as the heathen do : for they think that they shall be heard for their *much* speaking.

Be not *ye* therefore like unto *them* : for your Father knoweth what things ye have need of, before ye ask him.

After this manner therefore pray ye :

LORD'S PRAYER RECITED.

After the prayer the teacher reads:

For—if *ye forgive men their trespasses*, your heavenly Father will *also* forgive you :

But if *ye* forgive *not* men their trespasses, *neither* will your Father forgive *your* trespasses.

LORD'S PRAYER.

HYMN.

When the morn is bright and fair,
When sweet songsters charm the air,
I will lift my voice in prayer,
I will seek my Father ;
Lest my feet should go astray,
From His pure and perfect way ;
Lest I grieve Him as I may
I will seek my Father.

When the evening sun is red,
When each blossom droops its head,
Kneeling low beside my bed,
I will seek my Father,
That I slumber in his care,
Shielded from each harmful snare ;
And for life or death prepare ;
I will seek my Father.

From the Triumph.

GENERAL EXERCISES.

I.

SONG.

MARCHING THROUGH GEORGIA.

Bring the good old bugle, boys !　We'll sing another
　　song,
　Sing it with a spirit that will start the world along.
Sing it as we used to sing it, fifty thousand strong,
　While we were marching through Georgia.

N. B.　As the children are singing the chorus, have them keep
time by striking the top of the desk with their open hand, as
one, one,—one, two, three, one, one,—one, two, three, etc.

Chorus.—Hurrah ! hurrah ! we bring the jubilee,
　Hurrah ! hurrah ! the flag that makes you free
So we sang the chorus from Atlanta to the sea,
　While we were marching through Georgia.

How the darkies shouted when they heard the joy-
　　ful sound !
　How the turkeys gobbled which our commissary
　　found !
How the sweet potatoes even started from the
　　ground
　While we were marching through Georgia.—*Cho.*

II.

THE EASTERN WIND STORM.

The teacher faces the pupils and holds out her arms with the palms of her hands together. As she separates her hands, the pupils make a sharp, hissing, buzzing sound between their teeth, increasing the volume as the teacher's hands go farther apart. By bringing the hands to and from each other, the sounds will lull and swell making a very good imitation of a wind-storm. The children are always delighted with this exercise.

III.

THE TALKING PERIOD.

The teacher strikes three distinct chords on the piano, or hand-bell if there be no piano. This signal is for perfect quiet. Next, nine chords are struck. The moment the children hear the ninth, they are at liberty to indulge in a lively chit-chat with, their immediate neighbors, or in any other way enjoy themselves. providing they are orderly, not, of course, leaving their seats. At the end of one or two minutes three chords are struck when the children are to become perfectly quiet.

Do not forget to praise the children when they take the signals promptly, and never scold when they do not; but repeat the signal until it is done to suit you. If a teacher says to the floor, "My, how nicely you took that signal! You obeyed as quickly as a regiment of soldiers would have done! The children will be really pleased. N ing pleases a boy more than to be compared to a soldier. Te... ne children a story about some soldier who was slow to obey signals and was thus the means of the battle being won by the enemy.

If you cannot find one in history, write a little fairy story of your own and tell them that.

IV.

SONG.

THE RED, WHITE AND BLUE.

This song is one that all children like, especially the girls. The chorus here given is one which the children will understand better than the original and if each child be provided with a little flag, which he holds at his side until the chorus is reached and waves it during the singing of the chorus, it will add very much to the exercise. Flags costing fifteen cents a dozen are sufficiently large for all practical purposes.

O, Columbia the gem of the ocean,
　　The home of the brave and the free,
The shrine of each patriot's devotion,
　　A world offers homage to thee.
Thy mandates make heroes assemble,
　　When Liberty's form stands in view,
Thy banners make tyranny tremble,
　　When borne by the red, white and blue.

Cho.—Three cheers for the red, white, and blue,
　　　　　　　　Hip hurrah!
　　Three cheers for the red, white, and blue,
　　　　　　　　Hip hurrah!
Our army and navy forever!
　　Three cheers for the red, white, and blue.
　　　　　　　　Hip hurrah!

When war waged its wide desolation,
　　And threatened the land to deform,
The ark then of Freedom's foundation,
　　Columbia rode safe thro' the storm,
With her garlands of victory around her,
　　When so proudly she bore her brave crew,
With her flag floating proudly before her,
　　The boast of the red, white and blue.—*Cho.*

V.

THE WESTERN CYCLONE.

This exercise is the same as the wind storm in number II, with this difference. In addition to the sounds made in that exercise the children stamp with their feet. Let them have a good time, insisting, however, on their being orderly. Never mind the noise. Insist upon their following your hands; which, when near each other, should be the signal for their feet scarce touching the floor, gradually increasing as you separate your hands.

The boys like this exercise very much.

VI.

MARCHING.

Three chords are struck on the piano. (Perfect quiet.) Next, four chords are struck; by which the children understand that they are to march. One chord is struck; the pupils all stand. If the pupils do not take the signals satisfactorily, the teacher strikes middle C and then C an octave lower, at which signal the children take their seats again. (The children sometime say when the signal is given, that the piano says, "*Sit down*.") On the other hand, if the children take the signal satisfactorily, the teacher begins to play a march, pianissimo, during which the children all mark time. (Do not let them swing.) At the option of the teacher she begins to play forte; when the children at once take up the line of march which has been previously designated. It is nice for the teacher, sometime during the march to play "Marching Through Georgia," when the children sing while marching. Next, change to "The Mocking Bird," and and the boys will join in with the whistling chorus. Whenever the teacher desires the children to be seated again, she plays pianissimo, and each child, as soon as he gets opposite his seat, sits down.

VII.

RUNNING EXERCISE.

Teacher gives the same signals as for marching; to stand, turn and take places on the line. When all are in line she says: "Ready, run." Immediately all the children begin to run on their toes, keeping as good time as in marching, and equal spaces between each scholar. The running may be continued until the children become tired, or they may be stopped at any moment and the running changed to marching. This exercise, when properly conducted, is exhilerating and the children always like it. The exercise may be varied by having the boys run one day and the girls the next, thus creating rivalry. Of course, each class will try to be the better one. Still another change may be made; the running may be changed to a gallop. Care should be taken in this, that the scholars keep space enough between them so as not to interfere with the one in front of them. They should not be allowed to come down on their heels as this makes the exercise too noisy. Teachers will understand that this exercise is for the younger pupils, five and six years of age.

VIII.

HAND CLAPPING.

This exercise is especially good, as it not only sets the blood to circulating, but demands strict attention on the part of the children, or the exercise is a failure. The clapping should begin and end simultaneously. This will take patience on the part of the teacher who must not become discouraged if she does not obtain immediate results. As soon as the children succeed in doing it right she may be sure that they are not only doing, but they are also *thinking*.

The teacher gives directions as follows: "Heads, shoulders, heads, shoulders, up," the children placing their hands on their heads, shoulders, or up in the air, according to direction. Again:

"Heads, shoulders, up, ready to clap," "*Five*," when the children clap their hands ; one, two, three, four, five. Again, "Heads, shoulders, up, ready to clap, three times three ;" as, one, two, three, pause, one, two, three, pause, one, two, three. Again—Heads, up, shoulders, ready to clap, two and three, three times," as one, two ; one, two, three: one, two ; one two three: one, two ; one two three.

Other combinations may be given at the option of the teacher.

"Hands on your heads, shoulders, up, ready to clap,—as many times as there are days in the week, months in the year, school day's in the week, classrooms on the floor etc." This sort of clapping requires much more thinking on the part of the scholars than the other, and is, therefore, a wholesome exercise. Those scholars who make a mistake and clap more times than the others should not be allowed to clap until, as you tell them, they have learned how to count ; this will make them pay better attention and remove the impression that this exercise is only play. The following orders will vary the exercise. Clap as many times as a half of eight ; the number of times you ought to be told to do anything ; the number of hours you attend school ; as many as a half of six, etc.

IX.

HEAVY CALISTHENICS.

This exercise is good for the pupils when they have become restless and drowsy. Seven chords are struck on the piano as a signal for the children to sit facing the aisles. *With their arms folded in front.* The teacher gives the word "Ready!" when the children begin counting. After eight counts, the one at the piano begins to play, "Yankee Doodle." The children all stand and after four counts sit again and thus continue rising and sitting in time with the music. Care should be taken not to continue too long so as to overdo, and the children should be cautioned not to sit down with a jar.

X.

LIGHT CALISTHENICS.

Six chords are struck on the piano. The children then understand that they are about to take the light calisthenics, when all eyes are riveted on the teacher who is to lead. The pianist begins "Yankee Doodle." The teacher leading, then takes up different groups as, placing both hands on top of the head, tapping gently in time with the music, thus; one, two; one, two, three. Next bring the hands from the head to the shoulders and tap as before. Then fold the arms across the chest; keeping up the time. Any movements of the hands that may be suggested to the teacher are admissible. The great value of this exercise consists in *never* giving it twice alike, which tends to greatly improve the perceptive powers of the children and trains to form habits of giving close attention.

XI.

THE THUNDER SHOWER.

The teacher holds out her hands with her fingers hanging toward the floor. This is a signal for the children to tap the tops of their desks gently with their fingers. After this has continued five or six seconds, the teacher turns her hands with the palms facing each other. This is a signal for the children to continue the tapping and give out the buzzing hissing sounds as in the "Wind Storm." In a second or two the teacher doubles up her fists; at which time the children use their feet as in the "Cyclone." This, when nicely done, is certainly a very good imitation of the thunder shower. If desired, the following little song may be sung by a chorus of boys and girls, during the tapping on the desks.

SONG.

Clatter, clatter, patter, patter,
  Comes the driving pelting rain,
Clatter, clatter, patter, patter,
  On the window pane.
Hear it from the roof come pouring
  Thro' the spout come gushing,

O'er its stony channel roaring,
  Down the hillside rushing,
Clatter, clatter, patter, patter etc.

Clatter, clatter, patter, patter,
  Let it come! we'll not complain,
Clatter, clatter, patter, patter
  Welcome! pouring rain!
For we know that April showers
  Now so freely coming,
Wake to life the sweet May flow'rs,
  Soon they will be blooming,
Clatter, clatter, patter, patter, etc.

Song Garden No. 2. page 163.

QUOTATIONS.

I.

The pupils alphabet should be used as follows ; The children are to be named A. B. C. etc., from A. to Z.; then during the opening exercises in the morning, or the general exercises in the afternoon, the teacher calls each letter. As soon as called, the pupil whose letter is named, stands and recites his verse.

A.—A boy who feels timid about doing anything mean, is far from being a coward.

B.—Be prompt in all of your school engagements, that you may learn to be prompt, in after life, in all of your business engagements.

C.—Conquer your bad habits just as you conquer a hard problem in arithmetic ; one exercise is as good as the other to educate you, in fact, the former is more important than the latter.

D.—Do not eat after your appetite is satisfied. We are more apt to overeat than to eat too little.

E.—Every time a boy lies he belittles himself not only in the eyes of his schoolmates but in his own estimation.

F.—First make up your mind what you desire to do then be sure it is right, then do it be it ever so difficult.

G.—Get not in the way of cackling ; even a donkey knows better.

H.—Hasty tempers break good resolutions.

I.—If ever unjust, be honest enough to admit it.

J.—Join hands with no one who loves not his country.

K.—Keep your pennies and you will never want for dollars.

L.—Laziness and carelessness are twins.

M.—Make no promise you cannot keep.

N.—Never resign a position until you have secured a better one.

O.—Object to being led into doing what you know to be wrong.

P.—Profanity never made a gentleman and has ruined thousands.

Q.—Quarrels are like eggs; they grow worse with age.

R.—Refuse to do a mean action; be it ever so small.

S.—Sympathy makes stronger friends than gold, silver, or flattery.

T.—The events of childhood will be remembered longer and better than any thing else. So live and act then, boys and girls, that in the far future, when recalling them, they will bring naught but pleasure.

U.—Understand yourself and you will the better understand others.

V.—Vain people are seldom happy, from thinking of themselves too much.

W.—When sweeping a room do not forget the corners.

X.—Xenophon's prudence, activity, and vigor made him a leader of ten thousand Greeks, when but a young man.

Y.—Yield not to the flattery of one whom you have reason to suspect.

Z.—Zeal, rightly applied, will make a companion worth knowing.

II.

The quotations here given have been selected from standard authors, for school-children of the seventh and eighth grades: or in other words, children who have been in school for seven or eight years. Care has been taken to keep them within the comprehension of such children.

It is also thought that they will be a help in indirect moral training. The teacher should select the quotation for each pupil. Pupils are expected to commit the quotation to memory and when called on to recite rise from their seat, take a good position, recite the quotation, tell the author and give a brief sketch of his life. See page 38.

III.

Ask each pupil in the class to bring in a quotation written by a man whose name begins with the same letter as his own name, that is, John Smith might bring one in from Shakespeare; Henry Brown one from Burns; Mary Dawson one from Dickens, etc.

Here also it will be well for the pupils to give a brief sketch of the author's life.

IV.

Ask each pupil to bring in a quotation the first word of which begins with the same letter as his own name; e. g., John White might bring in the following:

" Whatever you do, do with all your might. Work at it if necessary, early and late, in season and out of season, not leaving a stone unturned; and never deferring for a single hour that which can just as well be done now."

V.

Write the names of different authors on little cards, place these in a hat, shake them well and then let each pupil draw a card. The next week he is to bring in a quotation from the author whose name is on the card which he has drawn.

VI.

Ask each pupil to bring in a quotation from an author born in the same month as himself.

VII.

Write the names of the months on little cards, place them in a hat, shake them as in V. Each pupil is to bring in a quotation from an author born in the month which is on the card that he has drawn.

VIII.

Write familiar quotations on little cards. Let each pupil draw a card and the next day call on each one of the pupils to read the quotation on his card and tell who is the author. If this exercise is rightly used the children may be taught emphasis, inflection, articulation and pitch, as well from the quotations as from the reading book. It may in fact, take the place of the regular reading lesson as often as once a week. Omit the author's name on the cards.

The following are good selections for this exercise.

"If any one attempts to haul down the American flag, shoot him on the spot."—GEN. JOHN A. DIX.

"I had rather be right than be President of the United States."—HENRY CLAY.

"Liberty and Union, now and forever, one and inseparable."—DANIEL WEBSTER.

"Millions for defense, but not a cent for tribute."
—CHS. C. PINCKNEY.

"The Americans must light the lamp of industry and economy."—BENJ. FRANKLIN.

"With malice toward none, with charity for all.
—A. LINCOLN.

"We have met the enemy, and they are ours."
—COMMODORE PERRY.

"Don't give up the ship."—CAPTAIN LAWRENCE.

"An ounce of pluck is worth a pound of luck."
—JAMES A. GARFIELD.

"Whatever I have tried to do in life, I have tried with all my heart to do well."—CHARLES DICKENS.

"No bill of attainder or ex-post-facto law shall be passed."—CONSTITUTION OF U. S.

"No title of nobility shall be granted by the United States."—CONSTITUTION U. S.

"No person shall be a senator who shall not have attained to the age of thirty years."—IBID.

"All men are created equal."—DECLARATION OF INDEPENDENCE.

"Ours is the best form of government which has ever been offered to the world."—JAMES WILSON (Signer of Declaration of Independence.)

> "Long may our land be bright
> With freedom's holy light;
> Protect us by thy might,
> Great God, Our King!"
>
> —S. F. SMITH.

"Dost thou love life? then do not squander time, for that is the stuff life is made of."—BEN. FRANKLIN.

"Handsome is that handsome does."
—OLIVER GOLDSMITH.

"We seldom repent having eaten too little."
—THOS. JEFFERSON.

"Lost yesterday, somewhere between sunrise and sunset, two golden hours, each set with sixty diamond minutes. No reward is offered, for they are gone forever."—HORACE MANN.

"Father, I cannot tell a lie."—GEO. WASHINGTON.

"It is better for a city to be governed by a good man, than by good laws."—ARISTOTLE.

"No one has a temper so bad, but that, by proper culture, it may become pleasant."—JOHN TODD (Vt.).

"Howe'er it be, it seems to me,
'Tis only noble to be good."
—ALFRED TENNYSON.

"Blessed influence of one true, loving soul on another."—GEORGE ELIOT (Mary A. Evans).

"Labor to keep alive in your breast that little spark of celestial fire called conscience."
—GEO. WASHINGTON.

"It is not right or manly to lie, even about Satan."
—JAS. A. GARFIELD.

"It is well for us all to be as happy as we can."
—JEAN INGELOW.

"Be not simply good, be good for something."
—THOREAU.

"He who gives freely, gives twice."—CERVANTES.

"It takes a good deal of brains to be silent."
—JOSH. BILLINGS (Shaw).

"Lottery is the worst species of gaming."
—JOSEPH P. BUCKINGHAM, (Conn.)

"Be true to your word and your work and your friend."—JOHN BOYLE O'REILLY.

"Affection is the stepping-stone to God."
—DONALD G. MITCHELL.

"In great aims and in small, I have always been thoroughly in earnest."—CHARLES DICKENS.

"Passion and anger make a man unfit for every thing that becomes him as a man or as a Christian."
—SIR MATTHEW HALE.

"If we delay till to-morrow what ought to be done to-day, we overcharge the morrow with a burden which belongs not to it."—HUGH BLAIR.

"Be good, sweet maid, and let who will be clever;
Do noble deeds, not dream them, all day long,
And so, make life, death and that vast forever
One grand, sweet song."
—S. P. COLERIDGE.

"One contented with what he has done, stands but small chance of becoming famous for what he will do. He has laid down to die. The grass is already growing over him."—C. NESTELL BOVER.

"Health is certainly more valuable than money, because it is by health that money is produced."
—DR SAMUEL JOHNSON.

"Give me health and a day, and I will make ridiculous the pomp of emperors."
—RALPH WALDO EMERSON.

"The common ingredients of health and long life are:

> Great temp'rance, open air,
> Easy labor, little care."
>
> —Sir. P. Smith.

"The talent of success is nothing more than doing what you can do *well*, and doing *well* whatever you do, without a thought of fame."

> —Henry W. Longfellow.

> "To thine our self be true,
> And it must follow, as the night the day,
> Thou canst not then be false to any man."
>
> —William Shakespeare.

"In the gates of eternity, the black hand and the white hand hold each other with an equal clasp."

> —Harriet Beecher Stowe.

> "There is a strength
> Deep-bedded in our hearts, of which we reck
> But little, till the shafts of heaven have pierced
> Its fragile dwelling. Must not earth be rent
> Before her gems are found?"
>
> —Mrs. Felicia D. Hemans.

"A grave, wherever found, preaches a short and pithy sermon to the soul."

> —Nathaniel Hawthorne.

"There is a great deal of wasted happiness in this world."—Mrs. G. R. Alden, (Pansy.)

> "Oh, walk with God, and thou shalt find
> How he can charm thy way,
> And lead thee with a quiet mind
> Unto his perfect way."
>
> —A. Cleveland Coxe.

"Duty be thy polar guide ;
  Do the right, whate'er betide !
Haste not ! rest not ! conflicts past,
  God shall crown thy work at last."
                    —JOHN WOLFGANG GOETHE.

"God has given us wit, and flavor, and brightness, and laughter, and perfumes, to enliven the days of man's pilgrimage, and to charm his pained steps over the burning marl."—SYDNEY SMITH.

"Crafty men contemn studies ; simple men admire them, and wise men use them."—FRANCIS BACON.

"I think I have never thoughtlessly meddled with the happiness of another, however trifling it may be, however strange it may appear to me."
                    —JEAN BAPTISTE KARR.

"Every lie, great or small, is the brink of a precipice, the depth of which nothing but omniscience can fathom."—DR. READE.

"Yes, child of suffering thou mayest well be sure,
  He who ordained the Sabbath loves the poor ! "
                    —JAMES RUSSELL LOWELL.

"He who has the God-given light of hope in his breast, can help on many others in this world's darkness, not to his own loss, but to his precious gain."
                    —HENRY WARD BEECHER.

"Habit is a cable ; we weave a thread of it every day, and at last we cannot break it."—HORACE MANN.

"Cheery people. O, the comfort of them ! There is but one thing like them—that is sunshine."
                    —MRS. HELEN HUNT JACKSON (H. H.).

"Better tenfold, to be sinned against than sinning."
—MISS MULOCK.

"What qualities are there for which a man gets so speedy a return of applause, as those of bodily superiority, activity and valor?"—WM. M. THACKERAY.

"Whatsoever thy hand findeth to do, do it with thy might."—BIBLE.

"How idle it is to call certain things godsends! As if there were anything else in the world."
—ARCHBISHOP HARE.

"Strive not with your superiors in argument, but always submit your judgment to others with modesty."
—GEORGE WASHINGTON.

"No true and permanent fame can be founded, except in labors which promote the happiness of mankind."—CHARLES SUMNER.

"The boy who is kind to his mother, will be glad to remember it when he becomes a man."
—From "SELECTED WORDS."

"If men wish to be held in esteem, they must associate with those only who are estimable."
—LA BRUYERE.

"Give us, O give us, the man who sings at his work! He will do more in the same time—he will do it better—he will persevere longer."—T. CARLYLE.

"A man should never be ashamed to own he has been in the wrong, which is but saying, in other words, that he is wiser to-day than he was yesterday."
—ALEX. POPE.

" At every trifle scorn to take offense ;
That always shows great pride or little sense."
—ALEX. POPE.

" A little fire is quickly trodden out ;
Which, being suffered, rivers cannot quench."
—SHAKESPEARE

" Joy and Temperance, and Repose,
Slam the door on the doctor's nose."
—H. W. LONGFELLOW.

" All may do what has by man been done."
—YOUNG.

" Half the ills we hoard in our hearts are ills because we hoard them."—BARRY CORNWALL.

"Do what conscience says is right ;
Do what reason says is best ;
Do with willing mind and heart ;
Do your duty and be blest."
—J. G. WHITTIER.

"Beware, so long as you live, of judging men by their outward appearance."—LA FONTAINE.

" We may not be wise as a Solon,
We may not be rich as the Jew,
Or as grand as a king or a sultan,
But let us be honest and true."
—C. H. HEATH, (Youth's Companion.)

"The last resource against temptation is prayer."
—JOSEPH S. BUCKMINSTER, (N. H.)

"The mate for beauty should be a man and not a money chest."—BULWER LYTTON.

" In prayer it is better to have a heart without words, than words without a heart."—JOHN BUNYAN.

"I have always despised the whining yelp of complaint, and the cowardly, feeble resolve."

—ROBT. BURNS.

" People seldom improve when they have no other model but themselves to copy."—OLIVER GOLDSMITH.

" Envious of none, I am determined to be pleased with all ; and, this being the order of my march, I will move gently down the stream of life until I sleep with my fathers."—GEORGE WASHINGTON.

"An able man shows his spirit by gentle words and resolute action ; he is neither hot nor timid."

—CHESTERFIELD.

" Ability wins us the esteem of the true men ; luck that of the people."—LA ROCHEFOUCAULD.

" When we cannot act as we wish, we must act as we can."—TERENCE.

" We must always be doing or suffering."

—ZIMMERMAN.

" Think that day lost whose low descending sun
Views from thy hand no noble action done."

—JACOB ROBART.

" Never do an act of which you doubt the justice or propriety."—LATIN.

" They never fail who die in a great cause."

—LORD BYRON.

" No life is pleasing to God, that is not useful to man."—JOHN HAWKESWORTH.

"Love will beget love ; a wish to be at peace, will keep you in peace. You can overcome evil with good. There is no other way."—WILLIAM LADD.

"Truth is so loyal to itself that it will not suffer distortion, even for the apparent purpose of doing God service. It can no more be swerved than God can!"
—WILLIAM HAWLEY SMITH.

"I believe that in the long run the right side will be the strong side."—JAS. A. GARFIELD.

"Oh how hard it is to die, and not to be able to leave the world any better for one's little life in it."
—ABRAHAM LINCOLN.

"Something noble, something good, something pure, something manly, something godlike, is knocked off a man every time he gets drunk or stoops to sin through forgetfulness of God."—JOHN B. GOUGH.

"Buy what thou hast no need of, and ere long thou shalt sell thy necessaries."—BENJ. FRANKLIN.

"A man can never be a true gentleman in manner until he is a true gentleman at heart."
—CHARLES DICKENS.

"Put not your trust in money, but put your money in trust."—O. W. HOLMES.

"Infidelity, true to its instinkts, works for the devil, and looks to the Lord for its daily bread."
—JOSH. BILLINGS.

"The men who are always going to do something big, would have done something big, if they had only been there, are never there; and if they are, they let somebody else do the work."—KATE THORNE.

"He is bold who feels timid about doing anything mean."—From "SELECTED WORDS."

"As flowers never put on their best clothes for Sunday, but wear their spotless raiment and exhale their odor every day, so let your Christian life, free from stain, ever give forth the fragrance of the love of God."—HENRY WARD BEECHER.

" Truth, crushed to earth, shall rise again ;
The eternal years of God are hers ;
But Error, wounded, writhes in pain,
And dies among his worshippers."
—WILLIAN CULLEN BRYANT.

"Hasty tempers break good resolutions ; and laziness and carelessness are twins."
—From " SELECTED WORDS."

" No matter what his rank or position may be, the lover of books is the richest and the happiest of the children of men."—JOHN ALFRED LANGFORD.

" How poor are they, that have not patience !
What wound did ever heal but by degrees ? "
—SHAKESPEARE.

" The heights by great men reached and kept,
Were not attained by sudden flight,
But they, while their companions slept,
Were toiling upward in the night."
—H. W. LONGFELLOW.

"Learn to live well that thou mays't die so too :
To live and die is all we have to do."
—SIR JOHN DENHAM.

" The Bible is the treasure of the poor, the solace of the sick, and the support of the dying ; and, while other books may amuse and instruct in a leisure hour, it is the peculiar triumph of that book to create light in the midst of darkness, to alleviate the sorrow which admits of no other alleviation, to direct a beam of hope to the heart which no other topic of consolation can reach."—REV. ROBERT HALL.

" We shall never learn to feel and respect our real calling and destiny, unless we have taught ourselves to consider everything as moonshine compared with the education of the heart."—SIR WALTER SCOTT.

"As for knowledge, it can no more be planted in the human mind without labor than a field of wheat can be produced without the previous use of the plough."—SIR WALTER SCOTT.

" He is great who confers the most benefits. He is base who receives favors and renders none."
—RALPH WALDO EMERSON.

" Could all the forms of evil produced in the land by intemperance come upon us in one horrid array, it would appal the nation, and put an end to the traffic in ardent spirits."—LYMAN BEECHER.

" To thine own self be true, and keep
Thy mind from sloth, thy heart from soil ;
Press on ! and thou shalt surely reap
A heavenly harvest for thy toil ! "
—PARK BENJAMIN.

" Live to do good ; but not with thought to win
From man return of any kindness done ;
Remember Him who died on cross for sin,
The merciful, the meek, rejected One ;
When He was slain for crime of doing good,
Canst thou expect return of gratitude ? "
—GEO. W. BETHUNE.

" The plan of salvation makes the prospect of death not only peaceful but joyful."—JOHN G. C. BRAINARD.

" I must submit all my hopes and fears to an overruling Providence, in which, unfashionable as the faith may be, I firmly believe."—JOHN ADAMS.

"The Bible is the book, of all others, to be read at all ages and in all conditions of human life ; not to be read once or twice or thrice through, and then to be laid aside, but to be read in small portions of one or two chapters every day, and never to be intermitted unless by some overruling necessity."

—JOHN QUINCY ADAMS.

"Would you let loose the flood gates of every vice, and bring back upon the earth the horrors of superstition or the atrocities of atheism ? Then endeavor to subvert the gospel ; throw around you the firebrands of infidelity ; laugh at religion, and make a mock of futurity ; but be assured that for all these things God will bring you into judgment."

—ALEXANDER ARCHIBALD.

" If any man in earth either angel of heaven teacheth us the contrary of holy writ, or anything against reason and charity, we should flee from him in that, as fro the foul fiend of hell."—JOHN WICLIF.

"In getting of your riches, and in using of 'em, ye shulen alway have three things in your heart, that is to say, our Lord God, conscience, and good name."

—GEOFFREY CHAUCER.

" There are two ways of keeping a promise ; one is to make an attempt and fail saying to our contented consciences, ' There ! I've done my duty, and it is no use you see ; ' and the other is to persist in attempt after attempt, until the very pertinacity of our faith accomplishes the work for us."

—MRS. G. R. ALDEN. (Pansy)

"Of all the causes which conspire to blind
Man's erring judgment and misguide the mind,
What the weak head with strongest bias rules
Is pride—the never-failing vice of fools."
—ALEX. POPE.

"It is to Christianity alone that the world was first indebted for those noble monuments of charity and mercy which are to be found in our hospitals, infirmaries, and other similar institutions. Not a trace of them is to be found among the refined and highly cultivated Greeks and Romans."—SAMUEL WARREN.

"The moral instructor, who is anxious for the welfare of the young, must feel solicitous to induce them to shun the beginning of evils so destructive to their peace and welfare ; and he cannot fail to urge them to avoid every kind of indecent language.

In innumerable instances, the first step to ruin has been indulging in impure conversation."
—LAUT CARPENTER.

"Let us each make the best use of our natural abilities ; and, with the blessing of God, we shall arrive at some good end. As for fame, it matters but little whether we acquire it or not."
—N. HAWTHORNE.

"But I've learned one thing ; an' it cheers a man
In always a-doin' the best he can ;
That whether, on the big book, a blot
Gets over a fellow's name or not,
Whenever he does a deed that's white,
It's credited to him fair and right."
—WILL CARLETON.

"I call that man free who is able to rule himself. I call him free who has his flesh in subjection to his spirit ; who fears doing wrong, but who fears nothing else."—FREDERICK W. ROBERTSON.

"The most substantial glory of a country is in its virtuous great men ; its prosperity will depend on its docility to learn from their example. May heaven, the guardian of our liberty, grant that our country may be fruitful of Hamiltons, and faithful to their glory."
—FISHER AMES.

" In the all embracing scheme of the eternal Providence, no act, or effort, or aspiration of goodness shall be in vain."—LEONARD BACON.

" Kindness will *always* do good. It makes others happy—and that is doing good. It prompts us to seek to benefit others—and that is doing good. It makes others gentle and benignant—and that is doing good."—ALBERT BARNES.

" A man's usefulness in the Christain life depends far more on the kindness of his daily temper, than on great and glorious deeds that shall attract the admiration of the world, and that shall send his name down to future times.—ALBERT BARNES.

" Above all, let me mind my own personal work, to keep myself pure, and zealous, and believing—laboring to do God's will, yet not anxious that it should be done by me rather than by others, if God disapproves of my doing it."—DR. THOMAS ARNOLD.

" The object of a good and wise man in this transitory state of existence should be to fit himself for a better, by controlling the unworthy propensities of his nature and improving all its better aspirations."

ROBERT SOUTHEY.

"The most beautiful possession which a country can have is a noble and rich man, who loves virtue and knowledge ; who, without being feeble or fanatical, is pious—and who, without being factious, is firm and independent ; who is a firm promoter of all which can shed luster upon his country, or promote the peace and order of the world."—SYDNEY SMITH.

"I expect to pass through this world but once, any good therefore, that I can do, or any kindness that I can show, let me do it now, for I shall not pass this way again."—MRS. A. B. HEGEMAN.

"Deception, or willfully misleading another, for the accomplishment of a purpose, is, in our opinion, just as culpable a falsehood as gaining the same end by a lie expressed in words."—OLIVER OPTIC.

"The greatest man is he who chooses the Right with invincible resolution, who resists the sorest temptations from within and without, who bears the heaviest burdens cheerfully, who is calmest in storms and most fearless under menace and frowns, whose reliance on truth, on virtue, on God, is most unfaltering."—WILLIAM ELLERY CHANNING.

"There is a day of reckoning, a day for the settlement of accounts. All unpaid bills will then have to be paid ; all unbalanced books will have to be settled."—GEO. B. CHEEVER.

"Opportunities of doing good do not come back. We are here for a most definite and intelligible purpose—to educate our own hearts by deeds of love, and to be the instruments of blessings to our brother men."—FREDERICK W. ROBERTSON.

" The reason why people so ill know how to do their duty on great occasions is, that they will not be diligent in doing their duty on little occasions."
—A. W. AND C. J. HARE.

" God asks of thee works as well as words ; and, more, He asks of thee works first, and words after. And better it is to praise Him truly by works without words, than falsely by words without works."
—REV. CHAS. KINGSLEY, D.D.

" Not sweeter are the flowers that make your valley fair, nor greener are the pines that give your river its name, than the memory of the brave men who died for freedom."—GEO. WM. CURTIS.

" No post of honor so high but the poorest boy may hope to reach it ; is the pride of every American."
—JAMES A. GARFIELD.

"There are some things I am afraid to do : I am afraid to do a mean thing."—JAMES A. GARFIELD.

" Well, then," said I, "if God does not forsake me, of what ill consequence can it be, or what matters it, though the world should all forsake me, seeing on the other hand, if I had all the world, and should lose the favor and blessing of God, there would be no comparison in the loss ?"
—ROBINSON CRUSOE (De Foe).

"Only by losing ourselves can we find ourselves. How clearly does the divine voice within us proclaim this, by the hymn of joy it sings, whenever we witness an unselfish deed or hear an unselfish thought."
—LYDIA MARIA CHILD.

"I have been very fortunate in worldly matters ; but I never could have done what I have done, without the habits of punctuality, order and diligence."
—CHARLES DICKENS.

"If a person be passionate, and give you ill language, rather pity him than be moved to anger."
—SIR MATTHEW HALE.

"Speak well of the absent whenever you have a suitable opportunity. Never speak ill of them or of any body, unless you are sure they deserve it, and unless it is necessary for their amendment, or for the safety and benefit of others."—SIR MATTHEW HALE.

"I hope I shall always possess firmness and virtue enough to maintain what I consider the most enviable of all titles, the character of an 'honest man.'"
—GEO. WASHINGTON.

"True eloquence does not consist in speech. It cannot be brought from far. Labor and learning may toil for it, but they will toil in vain. Words and phrases may be marshalled in every way, but they cannot compass it. It must exist it the man, in the subject, and in the occasion."- DANIEL WEBSTER.

"In the world's broad field of battle,
In the bivouac of life,
Be not like dumb, driven cattle !
Be a hero in the strife."
—HENRY W. LONGFELLOW.

"Thousands go over the rapids of intemperance every year, through the power of habit, crying all the while, when I find out that it is injuring me, I will give it up!"—JOHN B. GOUGH.

" He who hunts for flowers, will find flowers ; and he who loves weeds, may find weeds."

—HENRY WARD BEECHER.

" The Lord hides away the seeds of wonderful, joyful life in us ; and we sleep and wake, night and day ; and they spring up and grow, we know not how."

—MRS. A. D. T. WHITNEY.

" The boy who confesses his sins every night has always the fewest sins to confess."—J. G. HOLLAND.

" The world is a looking-glass, and gives back to every man the reflection of his own face. Frown at it, and it will turn and look sourly upon you ; laugh at it and with it, and it is a jolly, kind companion."

—WILLIAM MAKEPEACE THACKERAY.

" To the inspiration of necessity, we owe half the wise, beautiful, aud useful blessings of the world."

—LOUISA M. ALCOTT.

" Once more : speak clearly if you speak at all ;
Carve every word before you let it fall,
Don't, like a lecturer or dramatic star,
Try over-hard to roll the British r.
Do put your accents in the proper spot !
Don't—let me beg you—don't say ' how ? ' for
        ' what ? '
And when you stick on conversation's burs,
Don't strew your pathway with those dreadful
        ur's."

—O. W. HOLMES.

" Teach me to love and to forgive."—THOS. GRAY.

" If the whole world should agree to speak nothing but truth, what an abridgment it would make of speech."—WASHINGTON ALLSTON.

" The idle, the ambitious, and the needy will band together to break the hold that the law has upon them, and then to get hold of the law."—FISHER AMES.

> " Oh weep not for the dead !
> Rather, oh, rather give the tear
> To those who darkly linger here,
> When all beside are fled."
> —MARY E. BROOKS.

> " And they are most unworthy who behold
> The bountiful provisions of God's care,
> When reapers sing among the harvest-gold,
> And the mown meadow scents the quiet air,
> And yet who never say, with all their heart,
> How good, my Father, oh, how good thou art."
> —ALICE CARY.

" It cannot but be injurious to the human mind never to be called into effort ; the habit of receiving pleasure without any exertion of thought, by mere excitement, of curiosity and sensibility, may be justly remarked among the worst effects of *habitual* novel-reading."
—SAMUEL TAYLOR COLERIDGE.

"God is our Creator, our Father, our Benefactor, and is such a Creator, Father and Benefactor as deserves our highest love."—JOSEPH ALDEN.

BOOKS FOR TEACHERS.

SUGGESTIVE QUESTIONS IN ARITHMETIC.

By W. M. Giffin, Newark, N. J. Handsomely bound and printed. Price 20 cents.

A series of carefully graded and progressive questions in Arithmetic. Not in any sense "quizzisms" or "test problems" but plain and practical. More than one thousand exercises are given, and the revised edition now offered contains the answers.

SUGGESTIVE QUESTIONS IN GEOGRAPHY.

By W. M. Giffin, Lawrence School, Newark. Price 15 cents.

This is the second of the "Giffin" question books and exhibits the marked originality of this well known and successful teacher. We confidently recommend it.

SUGGESTIVE QUESTIONS IN LANGUAGE.

By W. M. Giffin.

It is something outside the old rut and we think you will like it. Language work has been a prominent feature of the Lawrence School and these questions indicate the course pursued.

STORIES FOR COMPOSITION EXERCISES.

Very handsomely printed and bound. Price 20 cents.

Material for "composition" and "reproduction" stories is always in demand, and we present here, in a neat and attractive form, one hundred carefully selected stories.

OPENING EXERCISES FOR SCHOOLS.

By William M. Giffin, Newark, N. J. Price 25 cents.

A book of this kind has long been wanted. "Where can I get suitable selections to read as a part of my opening exercises?" is a constant inquiry. This book answers the question.

PRIMARY READING : HOW TO TEACH IT.

Boston method. Arranged by the Supervisors of the Boston schools. Price 15 cents.

The most practical work ever published on this subject. Thousands of copies have been sold. It has been adopted by cities and towns, normal schools and reading circles.

SCHOOL-ROOM AIDS.

SCHOOL-ROOM DISPLAY CHART.

Price $1.00.

Each leaf is bound in morocco, and contains two brass eyelets. The workmanship is of the best and the entire weight of the Chart may be suspended on a single leaf without the slightest injury. There are ten leaves. It contains nearly 56 square feet of surface for the display of school work. Its leaves are a dark rich blue, furnishing a fine background for the paper on which the exercises are prepared.

Thousands have been sold to teachers in all parts of the country and not one returned as unsatisfactory. It is strongly indorsed by teachers of all grades.

RAPID PRACTICE ARITHMETIC CARDS.

By J. Newton Smith. Price 50 cents per box.

These Exercises are devised upon a scheme, with special reference to the best interests of teachers and pupils, making it possible for a teacher to do in a given time, many times as much work as by any other method and give abundant practice in the fundamental operations for all grades from the lowest Primary to the High School or Business College, where they need exercise in order to become experts.

SHEPARD'S SCHOOL-ROOM STENCILS.

A new and attractive feature in school work. Price, Maps and Charts 10 cents. Miscellaneous Designs 5 cents.

These Stencils are invaluable aids in illustrating Geography, Physiology, Reading, Language Lessons, Writing, &c. The designs embrace Maps, Physiology Charts, Script Letters, Old English and German Text Alphabets, Birds, Animals, Flowers, Borders and other designs for beautifying the class-room. No artistic ability necessary; any one can transfer the outlines to the board and complete the drawing. A large and perfect map of Europe, 24 x 30 inches, showing all the prominent rivers, lakes, mountains and large cities can be made in *eight* minutes. Each Stencil can be used an indefinite number of times and only requires a little pulverized chalk for immediate use. More than one thousand designs now ready.

BUSY WORK.

ALPHABET CARDS.

For the Chart Class, the Primary School and the little ones at home. Price 25 cents.

Profitable employment for little fingers during school hours. Pupils enjoy them, they lighten the work of the teacher, and greatly assist pupils in learning the alphabet and to spell.

ARITHMETIC CARDS.

These cards are for "busy work" in number, and may be used in a great variety of *number games.* Nearly 800 figures, signs and combinations, printed on bright card-board, assorted colors. Price 25 cents.

Each box contains all combinations to ten, but an endless variety of combinations may be made up to one hundred. For silent work at the pupil's desk they will be found incomparable, and at the same time the child will learn to handle numbers readily, without thinking he is set at a "task."

EDUCATIONAL TOY MONEY.

Fisher's patent. Price per box, 25 cents.

This money consists of discs of very heavy cardboard made expressly for this purpose, on which are imprinted accurate impressions of the various coins in common use. Each box contains eight small trays which are removable.

NUMBER GAME FOR PRIMARY SCHOOLS.

250 Cards, in handsome box, containing combinations to ten. Price only 25 cents.

This game may be played very rapidly, so that even in a large class every child can answer as many as ten or fifteen questions.

WORD AND SENTENCE GAME.

About 400 Word and Sentence Cards, assorted colors, in handsome box. Invaluable for making children proficient in sight reading.

Very popular. Price only 35 cents.

SUPPLEMENTARY READING.

By Principal A. B. Guilford, Jersey City.

Easy Reading Leaflets.

Presents in a new and attractive way stories of child life that are within the limit of the experience of boys and girls of our schools to-day. They have been prepared with special reference not only to the feelings and fancies of little children but to simplicity and directness of thought and expression.

A novel feature in their construction is their preparation in detached leaves. Each leaflet is complete in itself. This plan affords to the teacher the opportunity of providing each pupil of the class with *just that portion of reading matter under consideration for that day, and no more.* They are an excellent means for the distribution of good reading matter at the *slightest possible cost.*

Set I.

Designed to follow any First Reader. Printed on durable manilla card. Mailing price per set, 15 cents. 25 or more cards of one kind, 1 cent each.

There are ten cards in this set. Each card contains a story complete in itself. The following is the list of subjects :

1. Little Tom and Hero.
2. The Careless Fish.
3. What is My Name?
4. What Mollie and Fred Saw.
5. Harry's Popcorn.
6. Little Bessie's Party.
7. Daisy's Kittens.
8. Two Little Runaways.
9. The Rude Boy and the Rose.
10. A Funny Doll.

Set II.

Beautifully illustrated. Designed to follow any Second Reader. Printed on heavy manilla card. Mailing price, per set, 25 cents. 10 or more cards of one kind, 2 cents each.

This set contains ten cards and twenty lessons—two lessons on each card —the stories of each card complete. The following is the list of lessons :

1. Happy Jack.
2. Mamma Cat, Spot, Dot and the Frog.
3. Captain Joe and His Troops.
4. More About Captain Joe.
5. The Flyaway.
6. Story of a Fisher Boy.
7. The Strange Bird.
8. More About the Peacock.
9. Jack and the Puppies.
10. Maxims to Copy and Learn.
11. Rob and May in the Country.
12. The White Swan.
13. Mary's Little Cow.
14. The Daisy Wreath.
15. What Santa Claus Brought Will and Grace.
16. On the Roof with Jerry.
17. Evening Lessons.
18. The Gray Squirrel.
19. What the Winds Bring and the Brook in the Hollow.
20. The Lost Lamb.

PRIMARY LANGUAGE AND DRAWING CARDS.

Reading of an interesting and suitable character, ever new, is the great want of primary schools. These cards have been specially designed to meet that need. They will be found helpful to teacher and pupil alike. Sets, I, and II, price 15 cents each : the two sets for 25 cents. (20 different cards in a set).

www.ingramcontent.com/pod-product-compliance
Lightning Source LLC
Chambersburg PA
CBHW022035080426
42733CB00007B/844